Many
ARE THE PLANS
IN A PERSON'S
heart,
BUT IT IS
THE LORD'S PURPOSE
THAT
prevails
Proverbs 19:21

Now
MAY THE LORD OF PEACE
HIMSELF
GIVE YOU PEACE
at all times
AND IN EVERY WAY

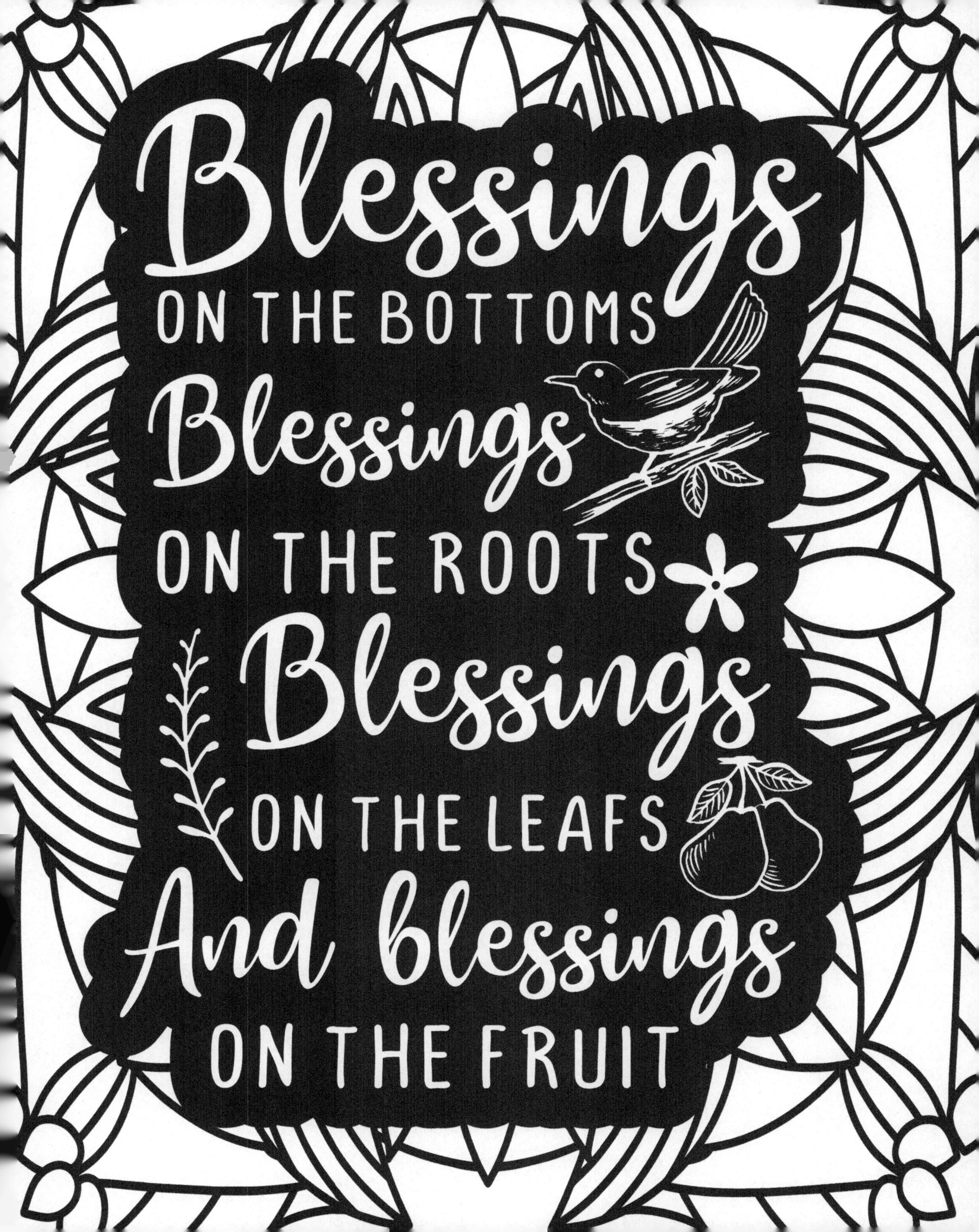
Blessings
ON THE BOTTOMS
Blessings
ON THE ROOTS
Blessings
ON THE LEAFS
And blessings
ON THE FRUIT

WHEN I WAIT
you strengthen
MY HEART

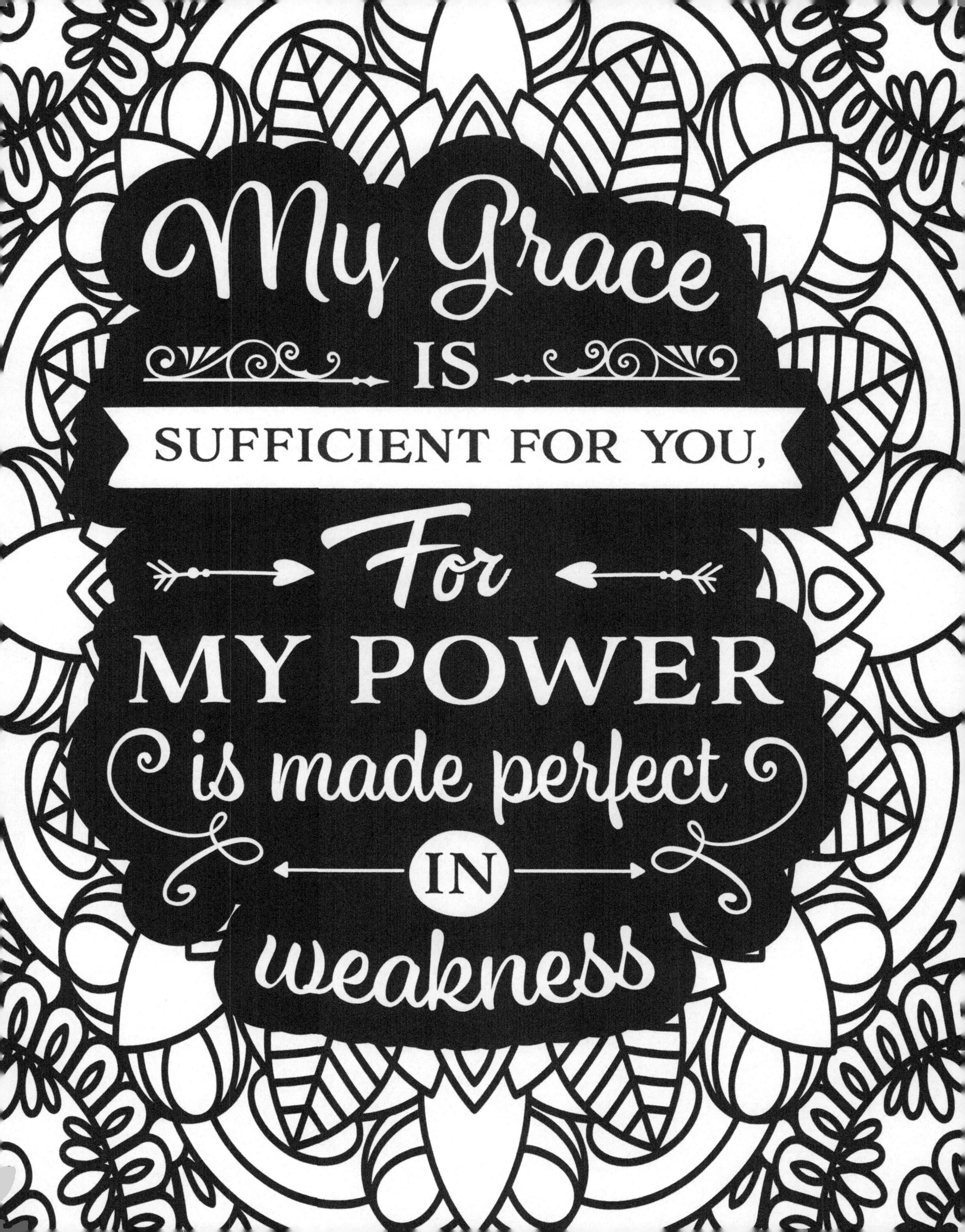
My Grace
IS
SUFFICIENT FOR YOU,
For
MY POWER
is made perfect
IN
weakness

MY GRACE
IS
sufficient
FOR
MY POWER
IS
MADE PERFECT
in weakness

TOO MANY
blessings
TO BE
ungrateful

FOR WITH
God
NOTHING
shall be
impossible
LUKE 1:37

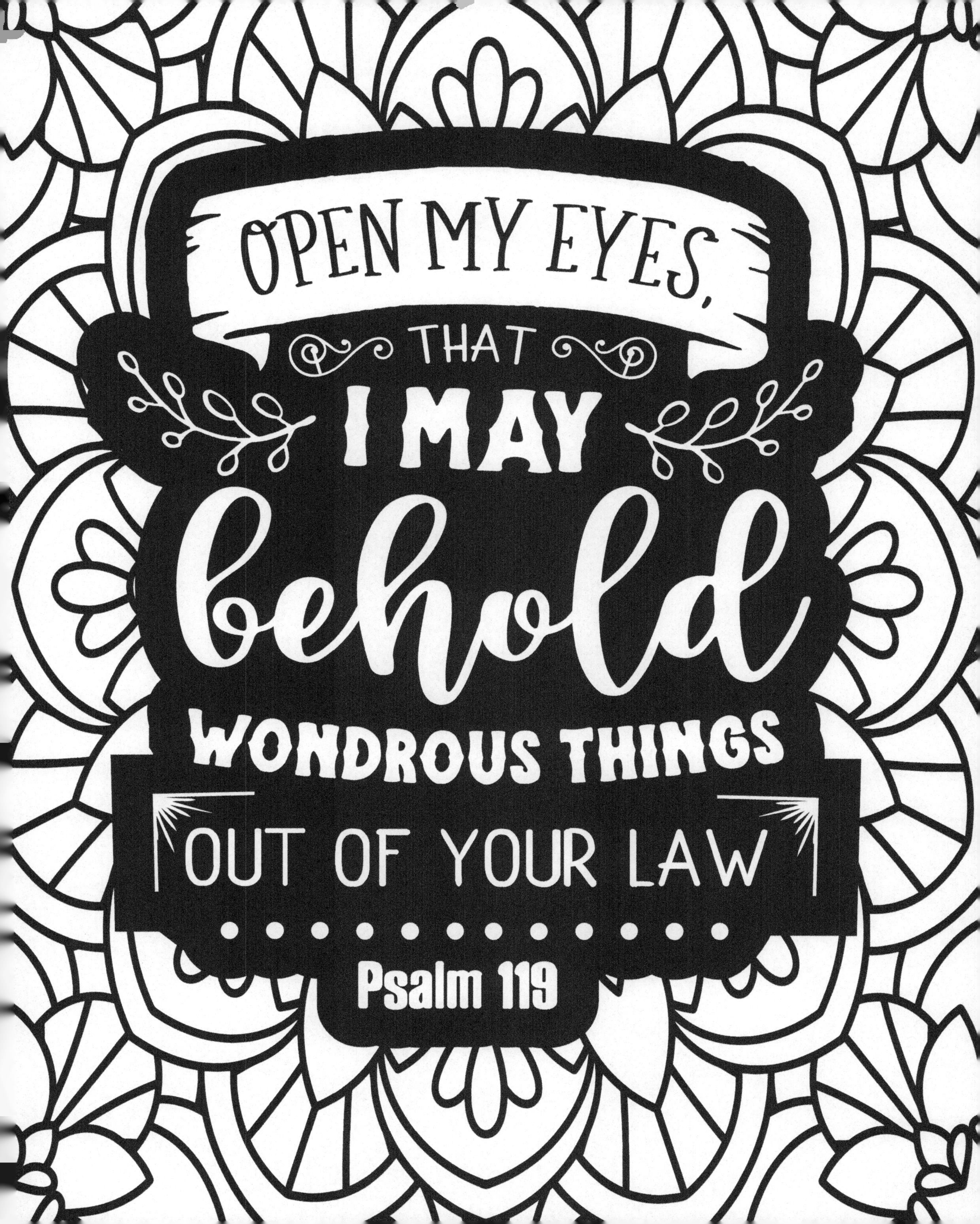
OPEN MY EYES,
THAT
I MAY
behold
WONDROUS THINGS
OUT OF YOUR LAW
Psalm 119

Rise
ABOVE &
beyond

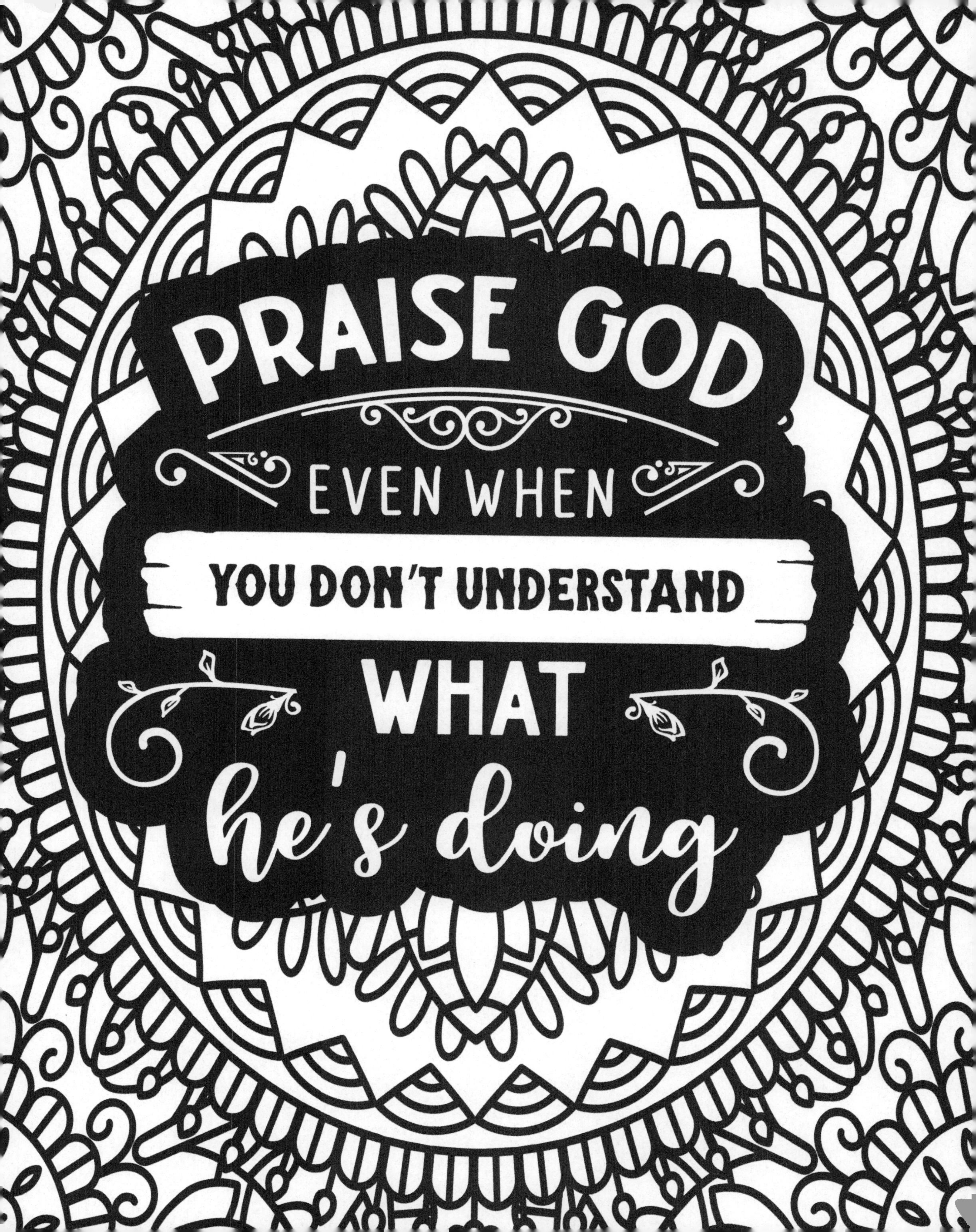
PRAISE GOD
EVEN WHEN
YOU DON'T UNDERSTAND
WHAT
he's doing

PRAYER
IS
the road to
HEAVEN
but
FAITH
opens the door

PUT
God
FIRST
and you'll
NEVER BE
last

Rejoice
and
be glad
for your
reward
will be great in
Heaven

Small seeds
OF
GRATITUDE
WILL PRODUCE A
harvest of hope

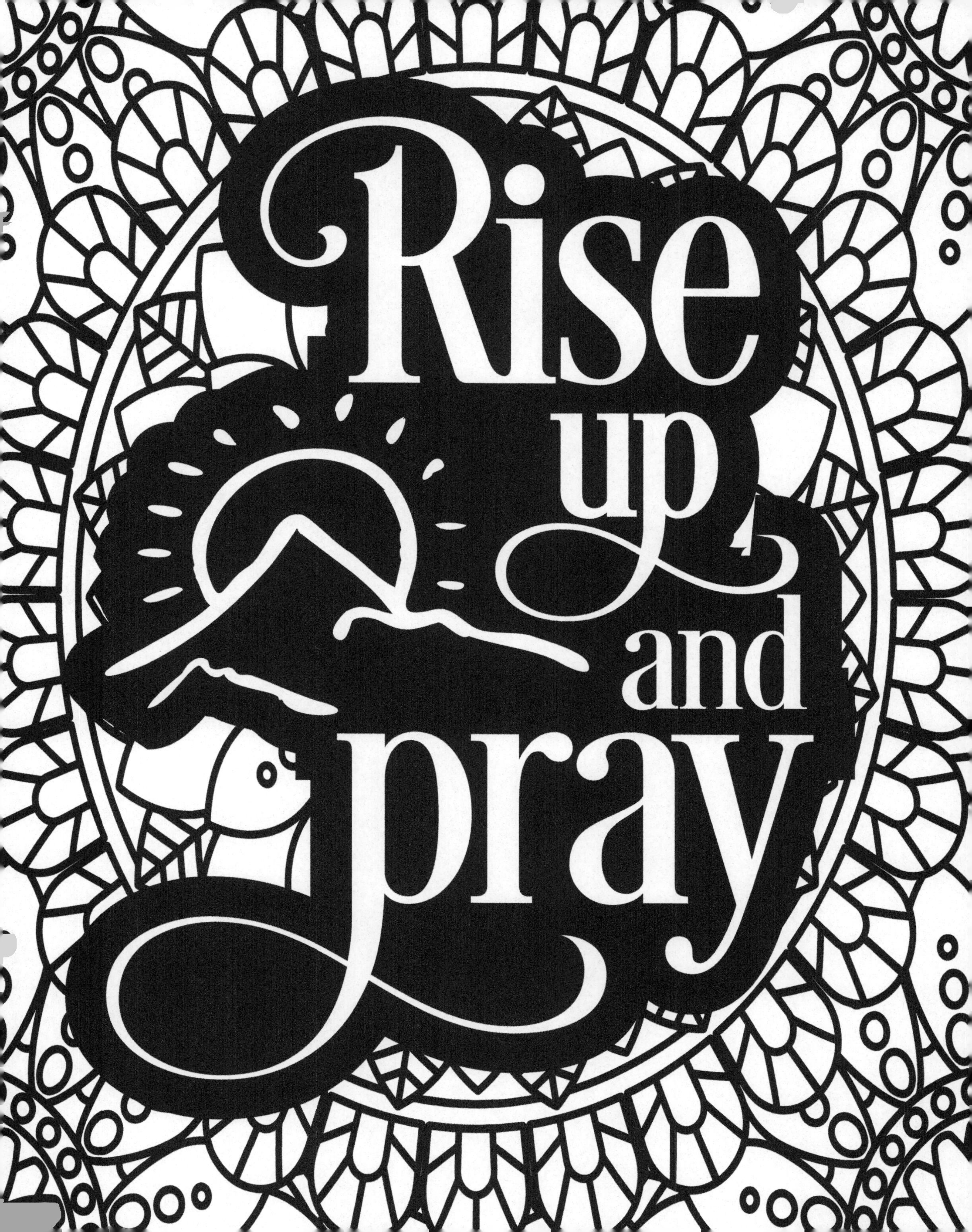
Rise
up
and
pray

Serve
ONE
ANOTHER
in love

Sleep in peace
TONIGHT
God IS BIGGER
than anything
YOU WILL FACE
tomorrow

ALWAYS BE JOYFUL
Never
STOP PRAYING
be thankful
IN ALL CIRCUMSTANCES

Storms
MAKE
TREES
TAKE
deeper roots

The best view
COMES AFTER
THE HARDEST
climb

THE
God
OF
Love
AND
peace
WILL BE WITH
YOU

THE
Lord
IS GREATER
THAN THE
GIANTS
YOU FACE

THE LORD
WILL FULFILL
His purpose
FOR ME
Psalm 138:8

There
IS A
BLESSING
IN THE
Storm

There is
ALWAYS
something
TO BE THANKFUL
for

Our Family
A CIRCLE OF
Trust
FOUNDED ON
Faith
JOINED IN
Love
KEPT BY
God

Trust
THE
process

Mightier
THAN THE
WAVES
OF THE SEA
IS
His Love
FOR YOU.
PSALM 93:4

When I am
AFRAID
I PUT
MY TRUST
in
YOU
PSALM 56:3

For additional interesting titles visit
On Mission Press on Amazon

For additional interesting coloring books
visit On Mission Press on Amazon